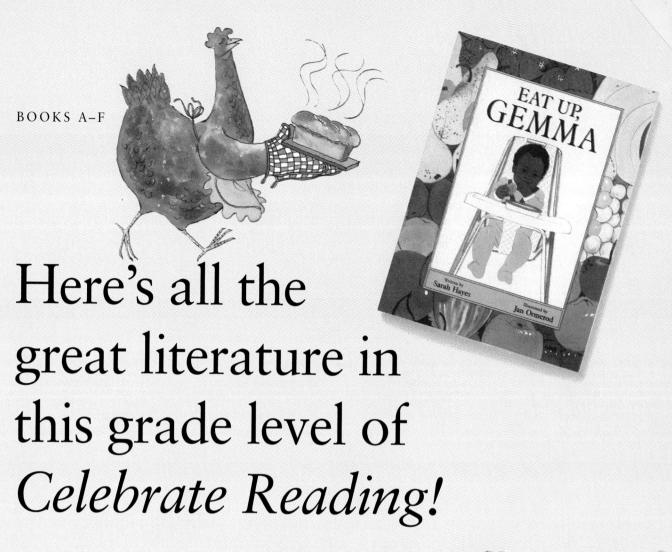

Here's all the great literature in this grade level of *Celebrate Reading!*

EAT UP, GEMMA

Written by
Sarah Hayes

Illustrated by
Jan Ormerod

The Doorbell Rang
by Pat Hutchins

ONE GORILLA
Atsuko Morozumi

THE NEW YORK TIMES
BEST ILLUSTRATED CHILDREN'S BOOK AWARD
WINNER

BOOK A

Under My Hat

Finding a Starting Point

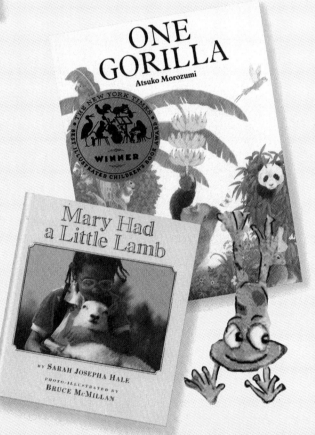

BOOK B

Hurry, Furry Feet

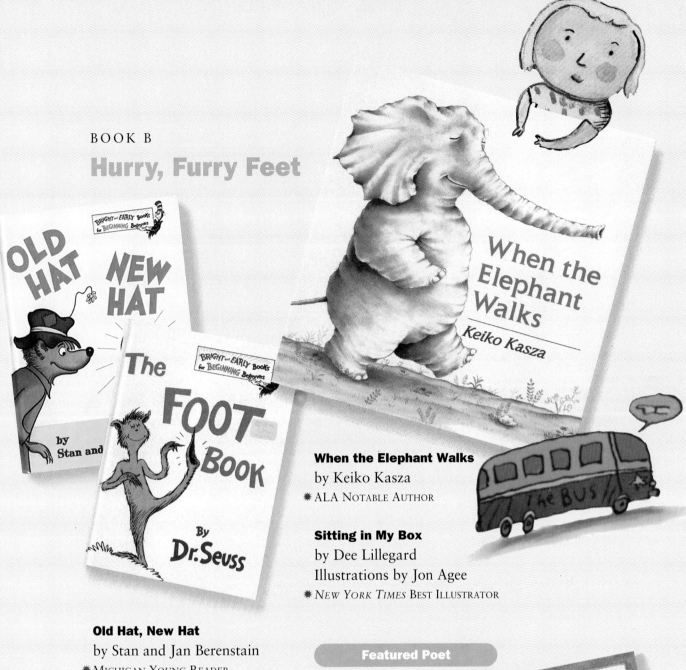

When the Elephant Walks
by Keiko Kasza
✳ ALA NOTABLE AUTHOR

Sitting in My Box
by Dee Lillegard
Illustrations by Jon Agee
✳ NEW YORK TIMES BEST ILLUSTRATOR

Old Hat, New Hat
by Stan and Jan Berenstain
✳ MICHIGAN YOUNG READER
AWARD AUTHORS

The Foot Book and
Hurry, Hurry, Hurry
by Dr. Seuss
✳ CALDECOTT HONOR ILLUSTRATOR
✳ LAURA INGALLS WILDER AWARD
AUTHOR/ILLUSTRATOR

My Street Begins at My House
by Ella Jenkins
Illustrations by
James E. Ransome
✳ PARENTS' CHOICE SONGWRITER

Featured Poet

Evelyn Beyer

Big Book & Little Book

The Wheels on the Bus
by Maryann Kovalski

BOOK C

Our Singing Planet

BOOK D
My Favorite Foodles

Featured Poets

Big Book & Little Book

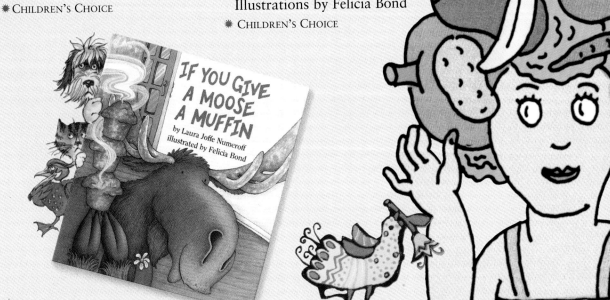

BOOK E
Happy Faces

A DELL YOUNG YEARLING
IT'S GEORGE!
Story by Miriam Cohen
Pictures by Lillian Hoban

Nathaniel Talking
by Eloise Greenfield
illustrated by Jan Spivey Gilchrist

Featured Poets

Eloise Greenfield
Karla Kuskin
Myra Cohn Livingston

Big Book & Little Book

ON THE GO
PHOTOGRAPHS BY KEN HEYMAN

BOOK F
A Canary with Hiccups

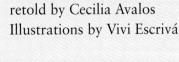

Big Book & Little Book

Celebrate Reading!
Big Book Bonus

It Looked Like Spilt Milk
by Charles G. Shaw

Jamberry
by Bruce Degen
✳ CHILDREN'S CHOICE

Skip to My Lou
by Nadine Bernard Westcott
✳ *REDBOOK* CHILDREN'S
PICTURE BOOK AWARD

Lazy Lion
by Mwenye Hadithi
Illustrations by
Adrienne Kennaway
✳ KATE GREENAWAY MEDAL
ILLUSTRATOR

The Cake That Mack Ate
by Rose Robart
Illustrations by
Maryann Kovalski

The Right Number of Elephants
by Jeff Sheppard

Our Singing Planet

Titles in This Set

About the Cover Artist
Donna Ruff grew up in Miami Beach, Florida. She now
lives and works in a small town near the beach in
Connecticut. She has illustrated several children's
books and books for older readers.

ISBN 0-673-81123-9

1997
Scott, Foresman and Company, Glenview, Illinois
All Rights Reserved.
Printed in the United States of America.

Acknowledgments appear on page 128.

5678910DR01009998

Our Singing Planet

ScottForesman

A Division of HarperCollins*Publishers*

Contents

Wild Things

I Like Music

Nice Job!

Wild Things

"PARDON?" SAID THE GIRAFFE

by Colin West

"What's it like up there?"
    asked the frog
    as he hopped on the ground.

10

"Pardon?" said
the giraffe.

"What's it like up there?"
asked the frog
as he hopped on the lion.

"Pardon?" said
the giraffe.

"What's it like up there?"
asked the frog
as he hopped on the hippo.

14

"Pardon?" said
the giraffe.

15

"What's it like up there?"
asked the frog
as he hopped on the elephant.

"Pardon?" said
the giraffe.

"What's it like up there?"
asked the frog

as he hopped on the giraffe.

"It's nice up here, thank you,"
said the giraffe,

20

"but you're tickling my nose
and I think I'm going to . . ."

21

"A-A-A-CHOOOOOOOOO!"

"Ooooops!" said the frog.

"What's it like down there?"
asked the giraffe.

"Pardon?" said the frog.

TALL TALK,
SMALL TALK

BY
COLIN WEST

You can have fun with the animal voices in my story.

When I read my story aloud, I use a deep voice for the giraffe. I make the word "Pardon?" very long. So, it's "'PAAAAAARDON?' said the giraffe." I make the frog's voice get louder and louder as the story goes along.

Why not try reading the story this way?

I hope you enjoy my story and pictures.

Colin West

Lion
by N. M. Bodecker

The lion,
when he roars
at night,
gives many people
quite
a fright!

The lion,
when he roars
by day,
scares people near him
far
away.

And when
he sleeps,
his lion snore
is quite as scary as
his
roar.

When You Talk to a Monkey

by Rowena Bennett

When you talk to a monkey

He seems very wise.

He scratches his head,

And he blinks both his eyes;

But he won't say a word.

He just swings on a rail

And makes a big question mark

Out of his tail.

Abracadabra

by Mary Ann Hoberman

GROUP 1: Abracadabra
The zebra is black.

GROUP 2: Abracadabra
The zebra is white.

GROUP 1: Abracadabra
The zebra is dark.

GROUP 2: Abracadabra
The zebra is light.

GROUP 1: Is it black striped with white?
Is it white striped with black?

GROUP 2: Is it striped from the front?
Is it striped from the back?

GROUP 1: Abracadabra
          It's ink over snow.

GROUP 2: Abracadabra
          It's snow over ink.

34

ALL: Abracadabra
Does anyone know?

Abracadabra
What do you think?

I Like Music

I Can Make

by Eve B. Feldman

I can make music.
Boom! Tap! Boom!
My hands can tap the beat.

Music!

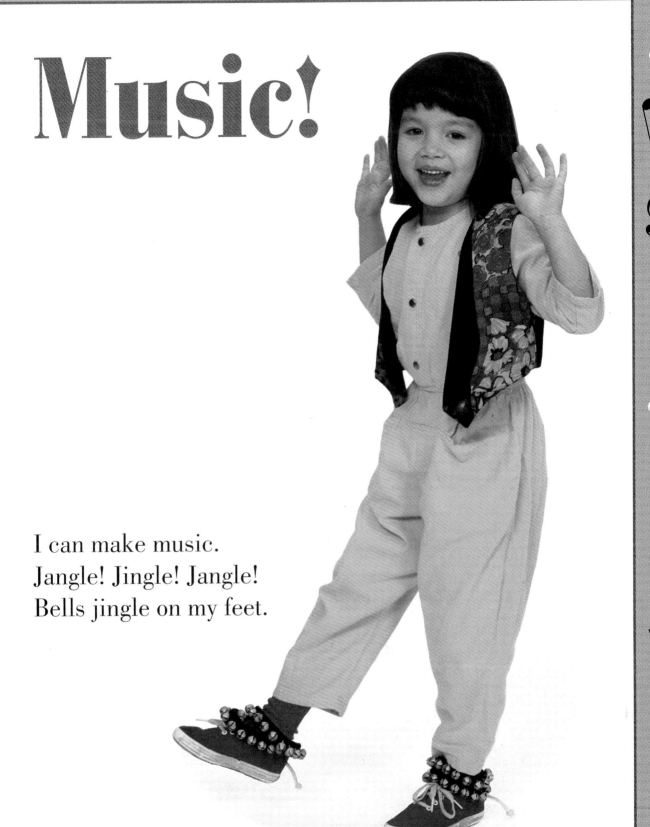

I can make music.
Jangle! Jingle! Jangle!
Bells jingle on my feet.

I can make music.
Toot! Blow! Toot!
Each blow makes a sound.

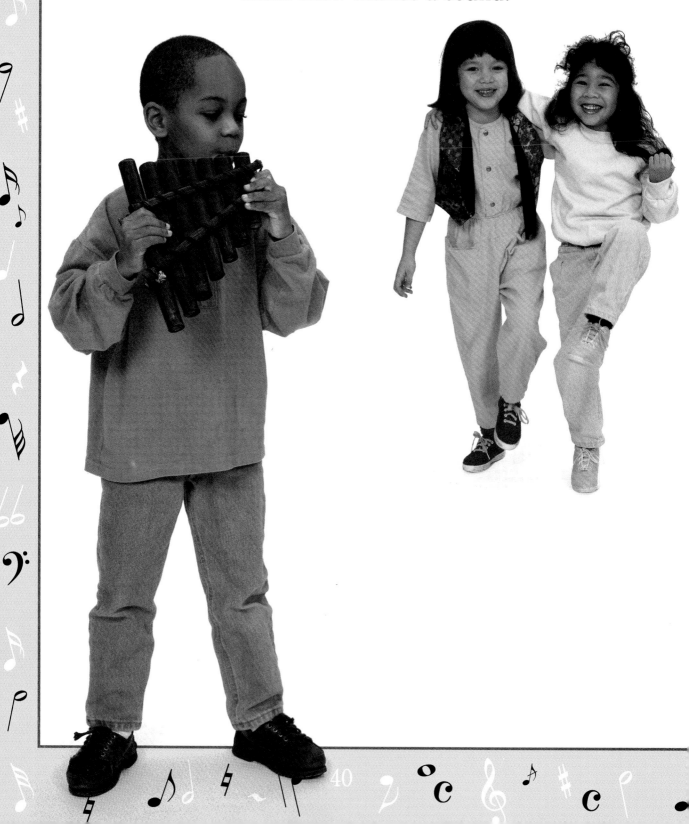

I can make music.
Rattle! Shake! Rattle!
I shake this all around.

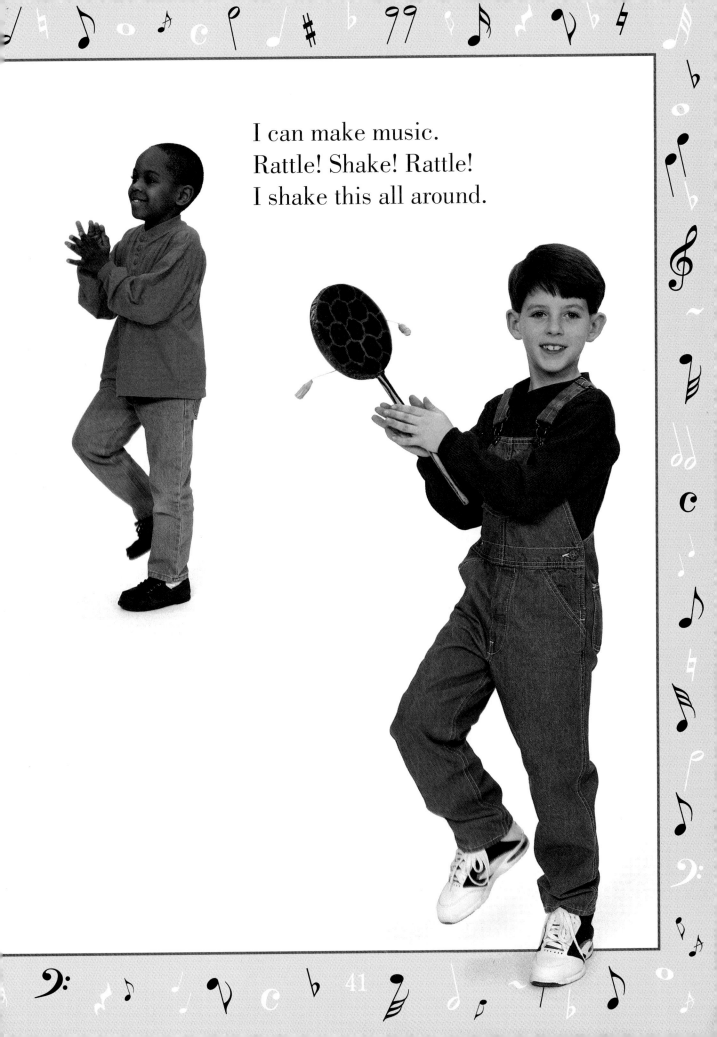

I can make music.
Pluck! Strum! Pluck!
My fingers strum the strings.

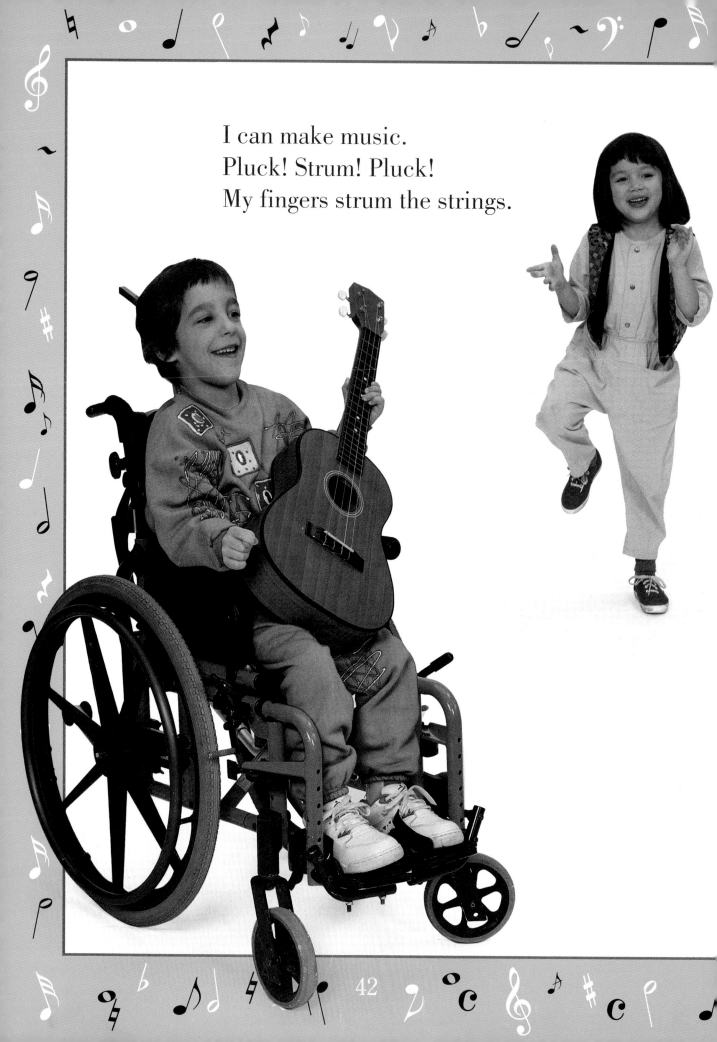

I can make music.
Ping! Tap! Ping!
I tap and the music rings.

You can make music too!

Try this.
Use a clean and dry container.
Fill it with dry peas, beans, or rice.
Seal it with tape and shake!

HAMBONE

Version by Cheryl Warren Mattox

Hambone, Hambone, where you been?
'Round the world and back again!

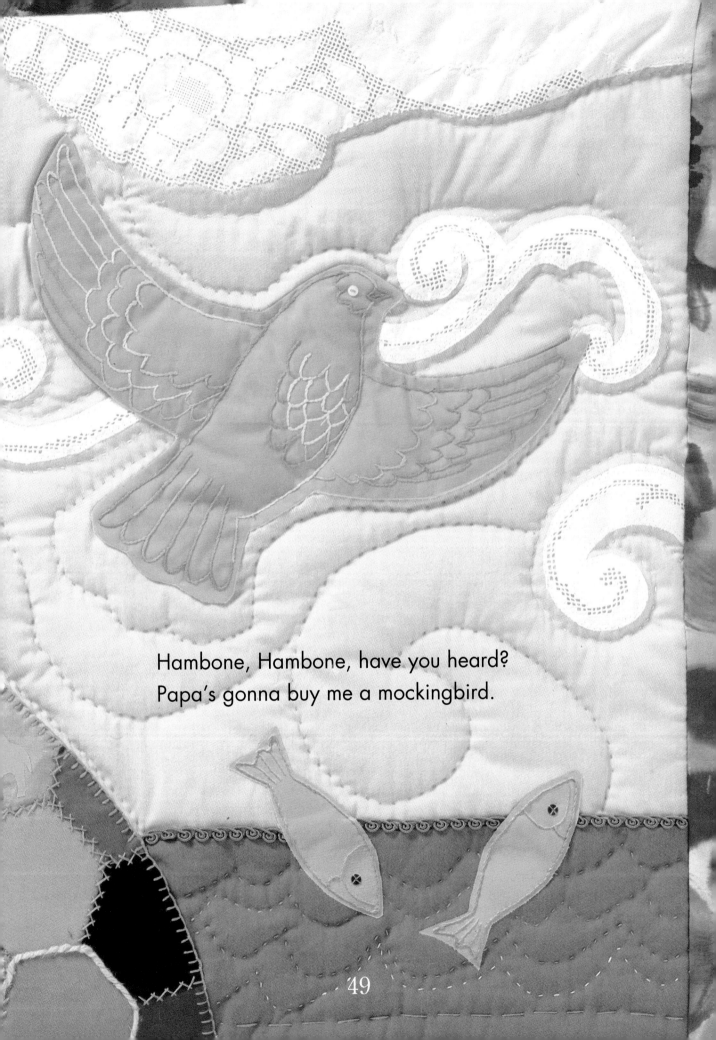

Hambone, Hambone, have you heard?
Papa's gonna buy me a mockingbird.

49

If that mockingbird don't sing,
Papa's gonna buy me a diamond ring.

If that diamond ring don't shine,
Papa's gonna buy me a fishing line.

51

Hambone, Hambone, where you been?
'Round the world and I'm goin' again!

The Little Red Hen and the Grain of Wheat

Retold by Sara Cone Bryant

One day as the Little Red Hen was
scratching in a field, she found a
grain of wheat.

"This wheat should be planted," she said.
"Who will plant this grain of wheat?"

"Not I," said the Duck.
"Not I," said the Cat.
"Not I," said the Dog.

"Then I will," said the Little Red Hen.
And she did.

Soon the wheat grew to be tall
and yellow.

"The wheat is ripe," said the Little Red Hen.
"Who will cut the wheat?"

"Not I," said the Duck.
"Not I," said the Cat.
"Not I," said the Dog.

"Then I will," said the Little Red Hen.
And she did.

When the wheat was cut, the Little Red Hen
said, "Who will thresh this wheat?"

"Not I," said the Duck.
"Not I," said the Cat.
"Not I," said the Dog.

65

"Then I will," said the Little Red Hen.
And she did.

When the wheat was all threshed, the Little
Red Hen said, "Who will take this wheat
to the mill?"

"Not I," said the Duck.
"Not I," said the Cat.
"Not I," said the Dog.

"Then I will," said the Little Red Hen.
And she did.

She took the wheat to the mill and had it
ground into flour.

Then she said, "Who will make this
flour into bread?"

"Not I," said the Duck.
"Not I," said the Cat.
"Not I," said the Dog.

"Then I will," said the Little Red Hen.
And she did.

She made and baked the bread.

Then she said, "Who will eat this bread?"

"Oh! I will," said the Duck.
"And I will," said the Cat.
"And I will," said the Dog.

76

"No, no!" said the Little Red Hen.
"I will do that."

And she did.

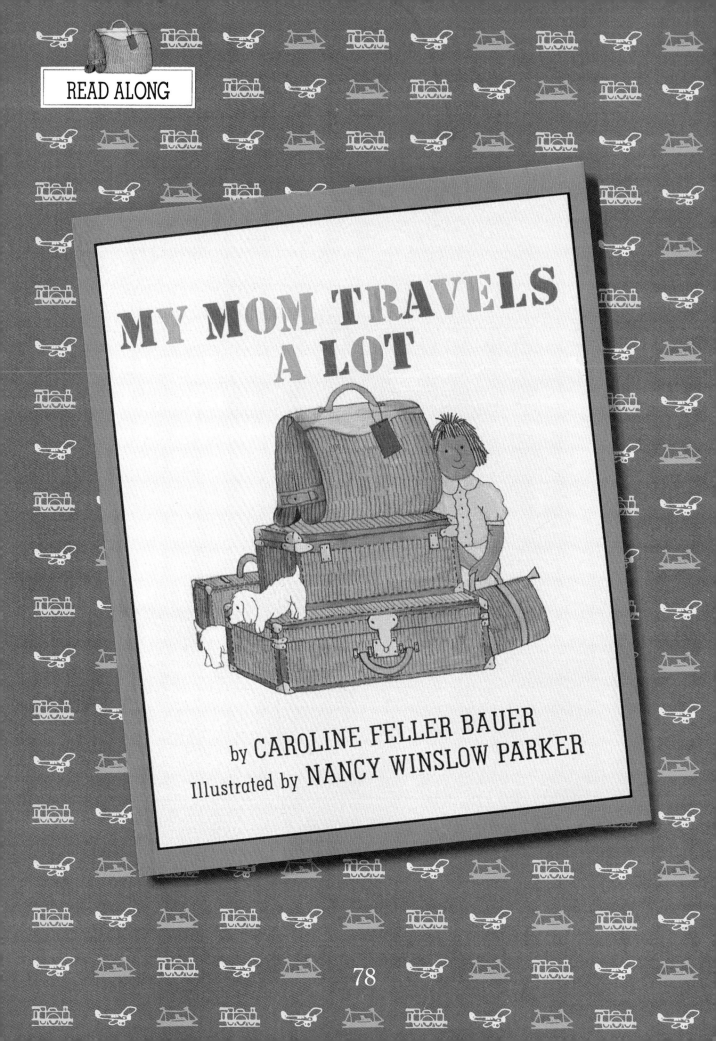

MY MOM TRAVELS A LOT

by CAROLINE FELLER BAUER

Illustrated by NANCY WINSLOW PARKER

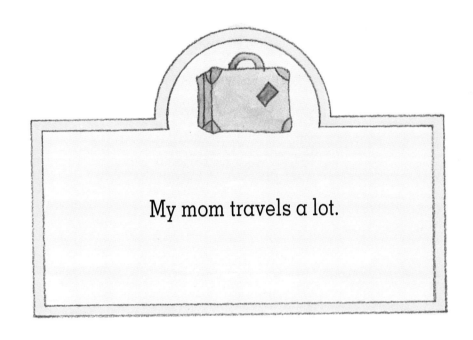

My mom travels a lot.

The good thing about it is
we get to go to the airport.

The bad thing about it is
there's only one nighttime kiss.

The bad thing about it is
Mom wasn't home when Susie
had her puppies.

Vet —
58 —
0753

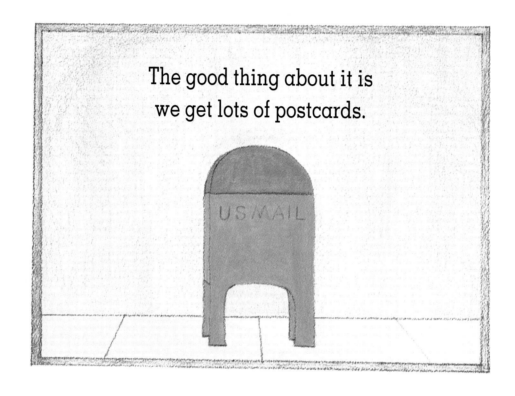

The good thing about it is
we get lots of postcards.

The bad
thing
about it is
Mom
missed
the school
play.

The good thing about it is
Dad and I eat out more often.

The bad thing about it is
I always forget to water
the plants.

The good thing about it is
I don't always have to make
my bed.

The bad thing about it is
Dad can never find my boots.

The good thing about it is
sometimes I get to stay
up late.

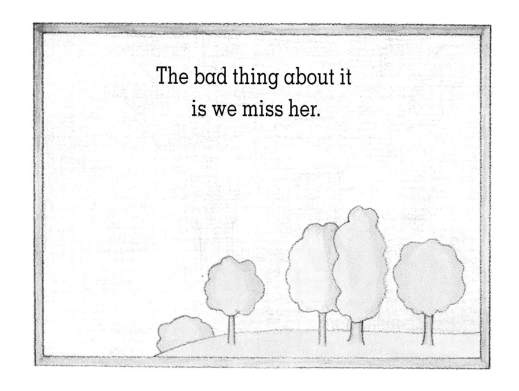

The bad thing about it
is we miss her.

The good thing about it is
we get presents.

But the best thing about it is

she always comes back!

This Is the Way
We Build a House

This is the way we build a house,
  build a house, build a house.
This is the way we build a house,
  as we work all day.

This is the way we saw the wood,
  saw the wood, saw the wood.
This is the way we saw the wood,
  as we work all day.

This is the way we hammer the nails,
  hammer the nails, hammer the nails.
This is the way we hammer the nails,
  as we work all day.

Tommy Meng San

by Belinda Yun-Ying and Douglas Louie

Tommy ran into the house.
"We had a call from Hong Kong," said Father.
"Grandmother fell and hurt her leg.
She is coming to stay with us."

112

"Baba, what can I do to make Grandmother
feel better?" asked Tommy.
"You can make her a card," said Father.
"I know that will help her feel better."

113

Tommy made his card.
Then he began to write his name.
He stopped.

"Grandmother calls me Meng San.
She'll like it if I write my Chinese
name," he thought.

114

"Baba, can you teach me to write
Meng San?" Tommy asked.

Father showed him the strokes.
Father said, "The first word, Meng,
means bright.
It looks like the sun and the moon."

115

"The second word is San.
It means mountain.
The word looks like a mountain too.
We want you to grow up to be as strong
as a mountain."

Tommy wrote his name on the card.
He was very proud.

Just then, Tommy's cat jumped on the table.

"Get down!" Tommy yelled.

Too late. Little San walked over Tommy's words.

"Little San, you spoiled my card.
Now what will I do?" Tommy said.

He had an idea.

"Baba, can you teach me to write my cat's name?" said Tommy.

Father showed him the Chinese words for Little San.
Tommy wrote his cat's name above his own name.
"Now the card is from both of us," he said.

118

The day came for Grandmother's visit.
Tommy gave the card to Grandmother.

"Thank you, Meng San," said Grandmother.
"And thank you, Little San," she said
with a big smile.

119

Do Your Best

by Belinda Yun-Ying
and Douglas Louie

We live in Seattle, Washington, with our two small children, Philip and Andrea.

We always tell our children to do their best. Our story shows how children can be proud of their work.

We hope our story will make you want to do your best too.

Books to Enjoy

D.W. Rides Again!

by Marc Brown

It is quite a job for D.W. to learn how to safely ride her bike. Her brother and father help, but they'd better watch out!

Nellie's Knot

by Ken Brown

Imagine a baby elephant tying a knot in her trunk! Read what she wants to remember.

Caps for Sale

by Esphyr Slobodkina

A peddler walks with a huge stack of caps on his head. One day he stops to take a nap under a tree. Look out, peddler, there are monkeys in the tree!

Baby Beluga

by Raffi

Illustrations by Ashley Wolff

Read this song about a baby beluga whale. Find out where he swims and who his friends are.

Who Is the Beast?

by Keith Baker

Does a beast have a long tail, white whiskers, and green eyes? What do you think?

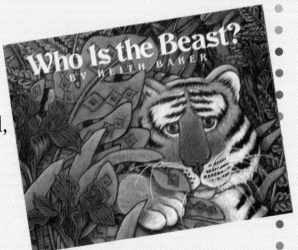

Daddies at Work

by Eve Merriam
Illustrations by
Eugenie Fernandes

Daddies lift you up. Daddies sing silly songs. Daddies fix broken toys. Daddies are busy people.

Pictionary

Workers

police officer

mail carrier

HOSPITAL

LIBRARY

doctor

librarian

Where
Things Are

behind

in front of

on

under

Acknowledgments

Text

Page 10: *"Pardon?" Said the Giraffe* by Colin West. Copyright © 1986 by Colin West. Reprinted by permission of HarperCollins Publishers and Walker Books Limited.

Page 27: "Tall Talk, Small Talk" by Colin West. Copyright © 1991 by Colin West.

Page 28: "Lion" by N. M. Bodecker. Used with permission of Margaret K. McElderry Books, an imprint of Macmillan Publishing Company, from *Snowman Sniffles and Other Verse*, written and illustrated by N. M. Bodecker. Copyright © 1983 by N. M. Bodecker.

Page 29: "When You Talk to a Monkey" from *The Day Is Dancing* by Rowena Bennett. Copyright © 1948, © 1968 by Rowena Bennett. Reprinted by permission of Modern Curriculum Press.

Page 30: "Abracadabra" from *A Fine Fat Pig and Other Animal Poems* by Mary Ann Hoberman. Text copyright © 1991 by Mary Ann Hoberman. Reprinted by permission of HarperCollins Publishers.

Page 38: *I Can Make Music!* by Eve Feldman. Copyright © 1991 by Eve Feldman.

Page 48: "Hambone," arrangement by Cheryl Warren Mattox from *Shake It to the One That You Love the Best*. Copyright © 1989 by Warren Mattox Productions. Reprinted by permission of Warren Mattox Productions.

Page 56: *The Little Red Hen and the Grain of Wheat* retold by Sara Cone Bryant, *Stories to Tell to Children.* Boston: Houghton Mifflin Company.

Page 78: *My Mom Travels a Lot* by Caroline Feller Bauer. Text copyright © 1981 by Caroline Feller Bauer. Illustrations copyright © 1981 by Nancy Winslow Parker. Used by permission of Viking Penguin, a division of Penguin Books USA Inc.

Page 112: *Tommy Meng San* by Belinda Yun-Ying and Douglas Louie. Copyright © 1991 by Belinda Yun-Ying and Douglas Louie.

Page 121: "Do Your Best" by Belinda Yun-Ying and Douglas Louie. Copyright © 1991 by Belinda Yun-Ying and Douglas Louie.

Artists

Illustrations owned and copyrighted by the illustrator.

Donna Ruff, cover, 1–3
Kiki Suarez, 4–9, 36–37, 54–55, 122–127
Colin West, 10–27
N. M. Bodecker, 28
Chris Demarest, 29
Helen Cowcher, 30–35
Maxine Friedman, 48–53
Don Almquist, 56–77
Nancy Winslow Parker, 78–109
John Jones, 110–111
Mike Reed, 112–121

Freelance Photography

Photographs not listed were shot by Scott, Foresman and Company.

Photograph

Page 120: Courtesy of Belinda Yun-Ying and Douglas Louie.